THE NOTEBOOK OF FALSE PURGATORIES

THE NOTEBOOK OF FALSE PURGATORIES

Standard Schaefer

2013 Chax Press

ISBN 978-0-9894316-6-8

Printed in USA.

Published by Chax Press
411 N 7th Ave Ste 103
Tucson AZ 85705-8388

Acknowledgment:
Some of these works have appeared in *Volt, Verse,* and *New American Writing.* Our thanks go to the editors of those journals.

for Corbett Bishop and Stapp Beaton

Because of the curvature of space all things meet at their extremes. What makes the next world infinite is that space there isn't curved but cyclic– as time is here. And time in the next world radiates in all directions rather that spooling out in fixed direction– time is a pulsation of life rather than a standard.

Malcolm de Chazal 1957

Got plenty of limitations, don't need any constraints.

Sisyphus

my companion in the skies
of death,
a cuckoo.

Fu Fu 1762

In the foyer, a bird tied to a telegraph machine, but not the sound of fluttering

The sound of a man alone in a round room typing with one finger one letter at a time

An ecology of alphabets and folded sheets

A stone for a sun, and its path is coastal

The moon grows close

Jump the moat

Round even to a faultiness in the round room. The walls are sore. Little rips in the flesh of them, as they are flesh walls. And beneath them real and steadfast matters.

Your trance or mine the only scene

Tragedy, then refrain

Repetition as structure verges on suppression, even dilution

And since I roam the arcades and barricades of a tonal intimacy

A tangible itinerary I cannot provide

Only these lyrical regressions and micro-intuitions
On how it is the rock won't roll and the stormer of peaks is still
upright

Even as we oppose them through confusion

Two or three degrees removed and stranded in the interruption

A florid athleticism for futile labor

Another hole in the chain link

It was in an age of transitive placelessness, and extreme tides

"a language received but denatured"

Then an era of earaches and with a compulsion to black out.

The big moment had entered the room.

A massive footprint, full of cabbage stumps and cod broth.

What was hard was taken as rigorous
Even indispensable to something soon

Unto loneliness, desperation and unto the partially revealed pat-
tern, design
if only in cycles so as to confuse the cops

Letters cut sideways and struck through with silence

The young ached for it, though outside passing the next table
a spasm of fatigue taken for longing —

sand blown moments against the carapace —

The anguished blur pounding the walls blowing the shabby whistle
looking for exit

Days spent boiling dictionaries in high noon of endgames and hel-
los

Recreation then decreation

As if in considering the position of things

Always on the side of leisure —

Fire ants and yellow inflatables.

The heads of wasps on children in towels.

One would have to say there is a small grass snake.

So as to explain the commodious hole.

In fact it would be only the hollow of the woodwind, and its squeak
would make everyone feel colloquial, so finally exposed—

For the sake of a public language, they would gather behind the air
conditioner and smother it with a bucket.

Eye to eye with the rooster's absence—

Gestation and incarceration the only furniture.

Nothing to start with, except the requisite exceptions

Before breakfast, a few pages of Suetonius

Then the constant urge to get up. The inability to do so.

And soon, behaving as if belief is required.

For a chaser, a broth of pearls.

Stones were said to be clogged with song. It was only ancient bodies falling slowly around the audience that, having been bitten, requested surgery to remove the marks, the sidewalks, even the sound of a beam of light had to be removed. The only clarity any one could stand.

It's out there and it stays there but we are its client

Distance prefigures abstraction some scarecrow back

Flies on the sleeves, a bat through a clump of shade

Leads some into counting cards and quoting Proust

Until an explosion of single events

Suggests simple ain't easy except when it is

Nerves through the grout

Forward only not forward enough that these words the only words
seem distant as the victims confirmed by the officials

Where distance is only absence gradually less frayed

Letters cut sideways and struck through with silence

Assume instants of exception and attraction
Assume the occupation of the victim

Assume survivors, especially infants

Assume the infant is horrifically effective.

That it is best for groups to cooperate and individuals to defect seems to render boredom dissent Gnostic in texture, curiously moist

How often it strays or restarts

Eels in the swimming pool, knees to the mat

Just as survival is an emblem of attendance

Against the figural and the notional

Autonomy even as inconsistency

Conflates the run in the stockings with the endless attempts at persuasion

Says the prisoner among his duck feathers

Wow, says duck, You really know exile

It's a social project hence long episodes of watering it on one side and turning it just so in the sun.

Appetite or august another day all window in a country shaped like a three-legged dog

Wow, says daughter, I really hate metaphors.

They are customs of abundance that like a bomb finally come to satisfy the arrangement of words on a napkin.

Interruptions in the stagnancy, a sharp surge in a friend's blessedly unfinished remarks

Another window for morning, another tube of vitamins
dissecting the holograph scrubbing its teeth

Acid miles

Redundancy poses as structure

The mouth of the canyon

Candlelight seven miles wide
and the airport bar

Eels in the swimming pool
Wires tied to the generator

Exaggerate the focus

"Were the churn to grant me another year or glimpse

Another tryst of the sort hay used to suggest

I would not have questioned what the pile of moths augured
            nor engaged the gardener in a discussion about what he
knew about the grounds

Settling instead for counting cards and quoting Proust

A purl of urgency, innovations in the arteries

For too long
            steered clear nonchalance of the atonal type

It lacked the kind of hypocrisy known to get things done

The thing is, though, the song intrigues me more than the breath
moving in and out of what's left of my chest"

Sisyphus from the satellite

Loneliness as immanence

      The play of extinction infiltrates empty space

      Covered in a shallow sea, unfettered static

      Wet shoes against a steel mirror

      Purgatory's perimeter— limbo's palpitations.

      The thrall of tautology

      War by identity

As Uncle Bob, said, "Tigers do not burn bright" nor does skin "twitter"
Like idioms and cuisine, both gnomic and simply carefully thought out
Reduced to music, sinkholes half-eaten pearls.

Progress is process and not the other way around

What comes when it comes

The rise of proximity against the heliocentric

"I don't have preferences
It will have preferences"

What can be accepted is here I keep records –

Listening softens up lightning

Light takes flight into phrases

Metaphors spawn wispy drinks

Immersion is the ceiling

But you are an oven of ash

What to include what to leave out

Which moon to choose if you do choose a moon

Consumed with waking
Or negotiating

One extra beat

As big as Mount Everest

I am told there is marine life fossilized at the summit
Some confuse with the braying in their heart

Up the mountain paths into the swirl of clouds, down the stairs through
the paper lanterns

Movement mobilizes the lull in the distance
Alsos and still-have-yous staff the museum

That in abeyance
leakage inheres

Light convenes the senses

But you persist— there is no skin, only scrolls,
and the light an atavism, almost a pineal accompaniment
so that between concrete and nerve, hollowed out muscles
syrup, purges, and frequent bleedings—

A raging stillness, just long enough to go unnoticed

And yet an amusing neutrality rampant

Nouns as large as them rare surprises

Defoliate events

Endeavored to build a conspiracy on an agreed-to-beforehand set of nos.
Mounting experiments near an exhausted thigh.

Perfumed in rain, waves crashing in their stern cocktails.

There is talk of it all too often being a matter of degrees.

But we, said the hostess, are not against intellectuals.
        We just favor the life of the mind.

No, we prefer a rich inner life. By which we mean divestiture.

A form of depravation so nuanced it obliterates the bones' alleged events.

Whereas nowhere else is the utmost promise
coincident the position shared with improvement
transformed by the recognition that recognition is mandatory
despite having fought or worked so long with knowledge
given reaction as treatment and commitment as empathy
and within a reasonable long-suffering correspondence,
accretion especially participation in the past
that is, in its current variation mindful the terrain
hardly coordinated with true vulnerability
on the part of the patterns, scapegoats, and apologies
four for metaphor and four against—
until consciousness is falsehood minus the music
and once more no room for you in the dull walls
same crevice last night same cruel music
of exile and repeated fumes, as if these
were the terms, as if the officious veneer
converged on an impending revelation
when the entire alphabet sings the pea-shucker's lament

The dry light in this crater, as if the light were snowing

Preened from the moon

A sclerosis in the metamorphosis

An afternoon almost divine in its emptiness, almost brittle

All morning it staggered and leaned through seven holes in the head

Black rain for paper, spools of worms for pens

A priestly static behind the husk

There's a crater where the knee is full of nettles
Reagan is dead and the Nasdaq is up

Image is a genre of hunger too intimate or quotidian

Deep time is a suitable distraction

Put down the purse and pick up the specimen

Dust rises and resettles three feet beyond the other side of the hall

It stings a little, then fizzes with a 'sorrow duly counterfeit,' as
Tacitus last night put it in his treatise on contingent forms of
upheaval.

Fissures in the anti-light   Muffled ledges of the elegy

Inspiration is only approval plus bees in the background

Those who are no longer here to agree
Could come to stand for the fact we are no longer candid

The pinpoint of the probe corrupt as what the whole field invades—

Those who crossed out the movement of the count
Those who came to become the Tsar

            And against a notion of empathy hinging on
                        suffering

A notion of vulnerability fragrant as the oysters nowhere in Tacitus

That flesh is sanction plus woods where a climate were preferable.

The music is the run-off

Heads or shoulders scattered across a weak uptrend

Time and fever

Quiver in the sulphur

Or the city of history
which is apathy

Around which diffuse tribes congeal

Peas on the breath

No, Mind.

A primitive accumulation

Analogue to the here

To live dispersed

So immune to the host

The elimination of the hearer

So unduly imputed

To a tenderness excessive as it is

Extracted

Density suffers from tightness

The idea of a stone

One diminished additional

Simple doors over simple doors

Rivulets around the archipelago
In a meditative stance

Take away the rivulets, take away the archipelago

Fluctuations in what won't sink

Mule hours and drift

Volcanic ash across the mayflies

Cleft shadows of silence and visitations

Another ferocious modesty

Hunkered beneath the sparks

And caramelized light

Because self-sufficiency is alien to language and spectatorship
common to the multitudes and presented as results

Things stand and are how they stand.
Then there is arbitrage between the uninvited and the unimpressive.
Heat dissipates.

And in place of the bite or the knife is the disappointment
no incision is needed or left.

Lower upticks, denser creases in the slope

Tides for a chart

The boots croak the uptrend is broken.

Things are how they are
or they stand how they are.

A woman deleted walks alongside
a man gone missing in the desert.

The first is a heuristic, so highly valued.

The second is strategic even if essentialist.

The third is something objectivity exaggerates.

The rest is the creaking from the podium

Boots exaggerate

On the first ascent the food seems too heavy.

It reminds them of the long wooden tables at the university, ceilings covered in drawings.

What was once cool dread in the grass is now a bouquet of hatchets.

Thus nature is the paraphernalia of time.

An afternoon spent dying from the idea of the cold
in a lecture on heaven at zero degrees.

Some say they are only crenellations in the lecture.

The clouds, that there is no heaven at all.

Only the hum and click of implements constantly restated.

Not watering not farming gathered mercilessly between three walls and one floor

And despite the feelings on the part of the floor.

The valley goes white or is abandoned to the design of four walls in a knot.

Despite the conditions or a cough that elaborates the conditions

Despite coming to enjoy the enclosure and behaving as if

Closure were required.

But if there is exaggeration, there must be consciousness.

And if there is consciousness, then there are questions.

What is the stance of the question?

The mere fact that we do not start from scratch.

Animality scours disorder

The body with its ruthless canals

Caves exhausted

The border is the horizon

Tone-deaf ocean after tone-deaf ocean

"The voices were a fine effect."

Covered in spores and technicalities.

In the middle, compression and impression humiliate knowledge

Elegies and apologies enter into harmony if not quite unity

Joy is otherworldly in the way both sides of the Sierras have their supporters

Tolerance is portrayed and sworn to fidelity.

Purgatory is tolerance welcomed out

Speed, settings, curious roads

Against the whole idea of a guide

Theorems in oil

Pulp

Incarnation

Microtonal with fits of enthusiasm

Amid the powder and vibrations

In the placental museum

On bent afternoons

In a room built of photographs

A clump of shade for the curvature of the back

Through the glass eye on the mantel, empire and immanent revolt.

It is not a crisis. It is a totality.

The hostess is a sonic boom.

The assailant is a black wall.

Excitation is the vacancy.

They drill even at night.

Where vacancy is desertion.

Against the dueling tranquilities of justice and abundance—

You proffer a more commodious form of exhaustion.

Once again as allegory but this for the pronouns and prepositions

Each of which leads to the fundamental infidelity that provides the only viable terms.

Men like pictures. Women prefer stories. East of saw dust south of the pasture

On toward Durango to kill Pancho Villa up to Montana to blow up Anaconda

Wheels stubborn as downtown means business.

Harmonicas are the official sources.

Each taut as the skin of a grape the knife no longer feels for

And divided by the piano tinkling on the opposite side.

Damp shadows of almost theological insight.

Politics, insists the hostess, has to be as crisp as clean prose.

She served the black pearl.

In structure, not compliance.

Chaos, says the dilated, is the big tent—

Intellectualism, control, cadence are just decorative if piercing light, posing empirical.

Durability subsumes eloquence.

Noise is different.

Wires are mnemonic like storm.

Lagooned in the prepositions, they will say, It isn't minimalism.

They skipped the transmission on precision, insisting it was only a matter of the meridians of your body, precognition

Another misty layer but the porous are embodied there.

It has come down to this.

Each purgatory is short but opaque as destiny is its own distraction.

Built on the strictly tonal, crawling with ants.

They were a blast and abandoned.

Grout on the weir.

But who among men are you from and what family or war?

And without generation, is there no corruption?

And without corruption, are there not certain things you just have to see?

Eager for the depiction of a danger unwittingly impeached

Torn from the book of purgatories

Again out of tune

But for just the once falsifiable

A decay in the affliction

During a lecture on fuel.

Black clouds oppose nonchalance

That chaos is not fiasco, only the long route
through the easy mark, and all over the white lines

A leg full of shrapnel or a belly full of fruit salad

That war is the health of the state and the state is blindness

That the alternative is lap dances or boot camp
up on Bald Hill

They're catching barracuda off Stinson beach
Running tripwires across the Rio Grande

But it's impossible to determine who is writing.

It's impossible to say who speaks,
what gender, what class, what war
as long as the bees blossom
or just hover
over "the quiet creaking of the masts"
or the figures in blogland
and their analogues in Hollywood

And yet I am almost certain

Personality is not community

Just the sound of the drill locking in place.

It reminds me faintly of Alaska, where the coast
I am told is crawling with tropical fish.

And to this someone adds a theory to aestheticize every synonym
for beauty.

But it's impossible to say who is saying anything
only that we tremble before the fumes
paced from the aperture and extracted from oblivion
Krieg lights weave across a tender career

I put on the facemask and stare at what's left of the barricades

Between the Bible salesman and the blouse of long braided hair
it's impossible to say what you're here for

You could be sipping mercury on the deck over a test site
or drinking rocket fuel from the Colorado

Instead, you come to tell me
rants are out

Here, we crank the disease

We who lay among the giant shadows
We who are but inappropriate comments

It's enough to make you take the kill fee, the French kiss,
the third turn in nine turns, and then stop at the snarling door
to bow deeply and swig the quinine

It's enough to shout May the best church win

Were it not that observation is humiliation where once it had been
involvement

All that is certain is we must oppose recruitment

Especially salvation, which is useless against the sweater on sale
or the surplus of reaction

Especially now that the skin has been revealed

All hype all the time.

In the center of the room is a translucent cube, and on each side, a film projection so that it looks like the cube has various colors of paint spread across each side. The paint is moving, changing colors. Through speakers you can hear nuzzling that you cannot see.

And as you stare at any one side of the cube, you can see nubs of flesh rubbing against the paint. For a brief moment here and there it becomes clear that what is moving the paint is elbows or knees.

"I want to go to the museum of fucking, actual fucking in a museum. Not a museum of erotic art."

Even Sisyphus moving on.

They liked the drilling rig towers—
They gave the landscape something to work toward.

There were waves of juridical diction.

There were people whose names would later be dropped.

So random, so lagooned.

Who will assemble the carbon, who will monitor the pressure
in the prelude to a chart?

Then dew beyond any viable harm, who will elude it?
There is so much dew. There are too many subtitles.

Mice regenerate from the pile of burning rags.

We went to a dank corner, watched the flames oozing against the
wallpaper.

A surge of fumes, paste.

Nationalism.

The same avant-garde as the last.

What the light does is lengthen the emptiness, thinning it out into ordinary sums, paler and paler colors until the molecules fade into a complete stop.

A road finds a beach where mist dissolves the crests of the breakers.

On the right, up to the far corner of the periphery
short buildings are washed out by a great wave of haze.

And still with a tendency to stray

Toward wherever it is one ought to say things such as these

Thinking of Tacitus and Suetonious perhaps beside a fire in winter-
time

Lying fully fed on a couch

Speaking slowly and eating chick-peas for desert

The lantern on low.

Steam then static.

But how old, good sir, were you when Lethe conquered you with
mead,
but don't say a word, don't even attempt to pay—

Only a theory of mercy is required—

Vast and empty as the overbearing will of the place
independent the economy of passions for which comedy was
invented—

Antidote to agency, quest, and hero.

Boldness to caution to boldness again

"Because war was to man what maternity was to woman"

Because a division of labor and a resurgence of inspiration,
especially disdain sustains whatever is the same or redundant or
current
with its turbines and defibrillators in the august flux

Whereas a hasty retreat as a sign of love—

Left foot to left square, right to etcetera

Progress is the mosquito's accomplice

Pleas and temperatures
Number and pleasures
Doled out and abandoned
To your afflicted powers
Really just the pleats
In the weakening place

Like serving peas until drowsily the fingers up the splendid neck
until just about now unthreaded

All of it as the impossibility of good judgment

When predicated on an audience that is against any notion of
identification, especially as tactic.

The war is only a summation

de-escalated clots of tower

phases and stages in the horses' retreat

but midday and massive

blood only an intimation, heat

a shameful effect of loops and force.

What had been called "involvement" becomes voice
in the noise of the day

Parabolic

But with munitions such as light through film

It seeks occasion, more often than not intonation provided absent
models, provided absent surly debunked absence

Although this too may be a triumph of management

To administer the routine so that it appears equal parts rest and
resistance

"You have the kind of community I lack and have had to replace
with meaningful work."

Involvement.

Having lived almost exclusively on electricity, static.

Identity is deterrence by other means.

Sense is virtually intractable, a solvent.

Where the throat is not an extravagance of lines.

As if accidents,
As if fragile,

Almost as if feverish repetition
had humiliated the raw material.

Only a place to rest the apparatus of absence—

What is behind and what is a head.

Dice that tell time.

Or the dice of meat rolling toward some idea of organization.

Nothing to stand on, nothing but the stance.

Asanas in an unhoused lung.

What moves beneath the skin is only the sound of knives colliding. The bees have moved on, the static has lifted.

Abundance barks an anthem and curls into a fist only an insomniac could avert.

Fuel and enchantment.

Scarcity makes its incision.

A tear in the critical distance.

There are forces requesting our march.

The telltale signs washed in light

It is January. It is noon in both directions.

It has become my understanding that purgatory is filled with some of the books you were not aware of are but had always sensed must exist.

Then talons.

Ascension perhaps glimpsed only through the hammer's bare calm.

Romance is revealed bald appetite.

Dead writers from different eras go there to correspond, only through gestures and sweaters or the same way the clock works, one bird at a time, swept out to sea all of it to the sound of typing.

A form of information discredited through encroachment.

Creation as dispossession.

It was represented by the voice of the child found beneath the pattern of stars distinct to that end of the park.

In this room, you get the sense that there's a goat in the next. You get the sense that the goat is eating a table. Everyone is certain this is part of the exhibit. No one knows how the artist has done this.

In the next room, there's a goat eating a table. You can watch it digest the sawdust because there's a window in its abdomen. There's one sixty-watt light bulb and a pack of matches, three sticks of gum, and a bottle cap visible. Pack of cigarettes, one big red ant and a butterfly. The music is that of mitochondria humming inside the veins.

A bird's wings turn into a letter.
The field is invaded by words.
Light is its gesture.
Time is what accounts for motion.
Propellers glom the skyline.
Ruins run through it.

There is a ceiling, but it is no guarantee of sleep

Whatever is etched is etched in the dark.
Powder is what's left of the dark elements.

Where it had been oceanic
It is now militant, flammable.

And what had been worth traveling at night
Is now a chore borne out in tactile qualities, irrecusable enigmas.

And by other words and other arrangements
Out of earshot, and far from the sun's scars.

How waxy the rain is written in the long stalk.
Spun into thread.

Against the figurative and the abstract.

The wind wasn't fragrant.

The air, perhaps, "mid-moth."

Vows to marrow and back to oath
Hashish hosts the lining underneath

It is impossible to say whether we are writhing

It is impossible to exclude the presumption
we have effects on others.

We assume captives.

Vows to marrow and back to oath.
Out of homage and into application

Not much sludge to book,

The ratio of sex to impatience

Still, the bones positively hummed.

No one mentioned it.

Or the long shadow of the tooth
flickering overhead.

Or the endless humidity.

As perception evacuated speech.

On to a stone. As if patterns
triangulate the voice. But not yet.

For now it is enough to say "afterwards"
And take off the head.
It says dance like you were broken
You draw two intersecting lines

Counter-clockwise the possibilities
Backwards up the staircase.
Left foot to right square.

That the secret is empty
And the earth a face.

That the face is a desire.
That desire is empty.
That the secret is earth.

That the other way works.

You'll find that'll be all.

That'll be all you find.

That'll be it.

The stars in that end of the park made a kind of hieroglyphics in triplicate. A kind of black like dark brown. It was a white horse that took us to it. It was the most volatile I'd ever ridden. In theory it moved like lightning, but the kind of lightning that lacked a cause. In theory and according to no particular privilege I once had such a horse. In reality, once you were on it, you belonged to it and not the other way around. Thus one love performed for two.

I was in a meadow, but it was made of cloud forms. There was a small sun without music. So it was early later, crossing the hills waltzing the elements in that classical style of bees. But they weren't bees. They were small suns. Things were slowing down. I was coming out of the bushes where I'd been curled up until there was suddenly too much light between the covers of the book I'd been reading in my sleep. I awoke to no goat and no table. No room after this.

Think, no, dredge.

The evidence—
Stars work the body

Anchored to the slightest infinities
bent like a fly's leg

stirring a damp spot.

Behind the vertical axis with the residue of experience—
almost of no value against the interior sensations but awash in low
instinct

The only cover was the radio, steaming.
Then gallant old ladies jingling their coins.

Two bees circled between the only authorities worth notifying
Structure crushed stillness but hiccups made us happy

Quilts trailed us, clouds walked off the perimeter

"Black" "Brown" "White"

The dog event.

Involvement.

An amount written on an envelope, each corner passed over a candle three times.

Drifted down the nearest stream.

A three-legged dog followed it so far, and circled back.

A wind wrinkled beneath parallel lines.

The rest was interviews with daylight.

A low wall dissolved as if through repetition
and against what was becoming an upturn in relics.

Content and intention gathering mercilessly overhead.

The pool became a matter of how you read the rain.

Often a bird beneath the feet
seemed to inspire a bright lamp.

Under it, the night went missing but lazy
as everyone meeting up in their sleep.

Canoes propelled by walking canes.

The late surfaced the itch
tried to depart.

As if to say, this far
and no further

Unless you strengthen your chest
and tighten your arc.

Afterwards we would come to speak the word "curfew"
over and over as we waited out the eclipse.

Take in the long drift, adjust the stilts
before following the bitten one last time.

What as a child had been the inside of a whale
is now a darkroom with mandarins.

"Poetry" is said to happen, distributed among fluteless nights
and the sway of the bridge, a wave gone long too pale.

It takes to the podium, but as a side effect of halogen.

The oval is white and rubbed in rosemary
and the spell is to banish debt.

The seats are equipped with projectors.

The audience is against the epic of description
through murmurs and by seeming variations
extending the most delicate, slender intuitions
and still there is the smell of the river bottom
amid the talk of phenomenology.

It is a kind of armament.

The hostess calls it prescience.

What had been called gathering beneath motive
and in its shadow was suddenly a few grains of sand
salt one more time so that when two are gathered
they are not the bitten, they are wind beneath the blazer
and wind some more almost Homeric

The drill of light.

Fist music triumphalism.

The forbidden as a spasm of paralysis.

Traffic seems to calm them and it seems
gunfire calms them, so there is gunfire.

But stripes move them.

And thrust before the orchestra upstart vicissitudes
or seated beside you an abscission at the base of the limbic brain
until surrounded by the late feeling that there's no reason to hurry.

There's no hurry here. No urgency.

A hint of the ruggedness to come.

They had started at the roof but without understanding it.
They projected supports, a title and some front matter.
They moved straight to sacrifice.
Someone brought forth a foot.

"Let's face it," said the hostess, "The familiar has run out."

But the foot was scentless and insensitive.

It was as if duration averred experience.

Someone says, "I have a recording of it"

But the presumption is it will be uninvited.

Therefore astonishing.

The only foot anyone could put any weight on.

They proposed de-carnation, and subtracted the question of resources but divided by the resources in question, grafting a plausible response to the inappropriate whisper on the part of apostates who argued for at least the symbols if not their accomplishments, while hardship and disfigurement took quotations trembling to bed.

But if watched long enough the story resembles a crumbling idea
names for hats, chrome for bones

The foot itself only in the preverbal

And if there is need for soup, fog will be provided,
provided one was entirely forehead
or a sequence of unpacking boxes or packing them
until the underlying cause was perspiration itself.

From context to contact some flesh-eating memory
of being, saying, going beyond "on"

Detached and spoke out

Against stillness, and for hemoglobin,
even an unsurpassable trance

But captivation doesn't work here.

Hobgoblins like vision and diction catch hold and go dim

Tender to cadence and reduced to the complex.

Their goblets full of moonbeams—

Derivations, spare generalities
were offered as protectors of liberties yet to be imagined.

Instances of light from somewhere
must remembered edges released
as if from a night spent in a series of calls
the curve of a woman's back blocks out the lamplight
the syntax of smoke, the roll of the hip is a rehearsal for rust,
in a photograph no one could place
with segments of needing all too often to be startled.

The dog's barking just as shakey as the scholar's attention
one final time through the text in some half-empty theater
behind the curve in an allegory about empiricism
as the square root of some decorative light
until it was as if one lung.

Then it was as if an orange sweater had come through town.

A boot ground in during the lecture on Arabic
or what won't rhyme and what won't be left out.

The scholarship and dogwork had to be paired back
but there was still talk of a reflex to kiss
followed by a lopped off fist still clinging to the knob.

The air thus fertile, as if punctured by syllables some scholarship
back. Just for a moment the audience endured the aperture.

Air through the creases, remarks ignited false
ten thousands just this once in place—

All that was needed to sooth the chamber
was an elixir of boundary-stones

They ordered a bottle of adrenaline and sat on a rock.

They discussed how the sublime seeks vengeance.

"Out with the alchemist, in with the welder."

Citations make music impossible.

They made a desert and called it peace. Who grants cadence to the oars and who fills the baths who goes eastward by force, westward to be free, who hath no ox, always in the circle that anticipates the circles to come

Nevermind the blooming or what goes on in other countries.

Forged from one side of an argument and left to maps and legends, territories of a second meeting, shutters.

"Obedience with legs."
Looks razor the curtain up

Loops prune the routine

Dendrite to the moment's notice

Mirror to the webbed edging

Rain to steam

Water to speed

The lens shattered dampens the beam.

Someone reaches a switch, hesitates.
Someone moves to the side.

Or a minute is stated as refused light.
Light clouds the acoustics.

Whether or not boredom discloses the divine

History rejects habitat

Form crumples stasis.

Heaven, it has been said, is filled with divorced women

And this morning a journalist who believes the distance to the next
switch is a question worth holding

If more private than an angel cutting her skull out

Thus associated with total clarity and exhaustion

Sight alarms proportion. Birds rise
to usurp the pings of the dead.

Dust is light and night is must

Ease an answer not worth the question

Courage, it is said, wanders even outside meaning
or the aesthetics of meaning, organize like a stupor

The archive inflamed surrounds a bifurcated silence

Balanced on a lumpy axis of hobbled shadow, and streaks gradually
flaking.

Frost.

Premonitions.

Phosphor, ether, whatever is left in the bulb, dims.

A map of insignificant stars.
An ear for excavation, an eye out for scraps
infinity hollowed out and enclosed in procedure
poached by agenda and without a face
shoulders indistinguishable from the horizon
but in the addenda are those who came to be counted
the same number of holes the same grain allotted
some with swans where they'd hoped for bodies
forceps, forced steps, echoes and abstraction
who do exactly as they do and are through
with writing through

Bruising, no, brooding was simply the muscle giving way
until nothing to drift

Through the scars and rumors of scars
heard from the scaffolding over the imploding flash.

The foot was replaced by numbers or the desire for numbers to
romance the steady-state.

Because there was never a market, subsidies sopped up the frac-
tions.

Loud was predictable and typed a bold face.

Wishes blurbed tradition.

Cronies pummeled integrals, only integers clawed out
through a funnel to a narrative refused.

Some words clotted along the way.

Parasite limped along an exquisite flaw.

The steady hand of false routine.

Clarity and its vengeance
scald a sterile line.

Antlers scrape in the darkness.

The spatial takes the vacationer out for a walk

Negation strobes non sequitur.

Space melts the kaleidoscope. A voice rambles.   An asteroid belt wanders the oral, the written, the experiential.

The invisible rings.

Dimension breaches typography.

Topography patrols the beach.

But the only cargo of the infinite is the dead moan.

Curtain after curtain, curfews and tight spots in the prisoner's solution.

The tides swell polyhedral and the vacuum is noisier than intended.

A rock is peeled to its first syllable.

Collisions crawl toward the white core of zero belief.

Stones cling to the lacustrine.

What is called sinking is most authoritative.

Authentic.

Totally monotonous.

The way letters speak to us.

Animism.

It offends everyone.

Mosquitoes breed beneath the surface of the eye.

Dogs bark the bend in the light.

Speech succumbs to perception.

The angler corrects his cast.

Enough of this for that and the otherwise back

Enough stone, scale, time wherefrom.

It is a frozen sun above

Or below and soon

Pulled apart by the static hiss and the anti-stone

That makes these tides all the more exalted

Though less and less moisture

More and more leisure and snailfat

What from here at least is too swollen with stones
For the war to ever breach it
Must be left behind with the compass

The ferns to their moonwater

And what the numbness attempts to describe.

A false impasse animates ink's silhouette.

Leave it all like the clear-cut and the moment longer

Leave the towering absence to its incessant descent

The marble wobbling in the mind to the little patterns
coming apart in our eyes.

I recognize the man across from us, who is neither wet nor dry,
only a memory of observable traits

When we speak to him, we will experience the presence of others
inside us studying the flight of fleas

It will be useless against the squeaks in our species or
the tongue wrapped in foil

It will be a fortifying of the position

                dust is light and night is must

        beneath these bulky robes

           two moths

    circle

        the only summer recorded

History being against habitat

                And the body being a communism

            of nerves and gimmicks

From here, it's wind all the way down, nary a moth.

The way alignment never was planetary.

Local is the real time, the relation between emotion and occasion.

It's not the good kind of tired nor the result stated one line below.

Echoes and restlessness notwithstanding.

It's simply the brute fact that there is no other place, so it is useless to apply satire, eulogy, or guile.

Tread the necessary fluctuations in emptiness or inexperience

Breathe a tenuous breath—a form of doubt posing as potential.

So it seems structure diminishes what had been life-like about demand A gnat for a guide on a path through the gnats bears the convolution to its source

That living is only the irreparability of constant exposure, especially impotence

Something must champion the non-existent, the uncertain, the interrupted.

But the room objects to the objects in the room

Pseudopods, larval bodies

Fungibility is what has been taken away

Selected by recklessness because only recklessness remains

Thus the sublime must be suggested, if not invoked, by the crude
edge of the iterations and reiterations that begin or began at the top
and devolved into real things then sounds not real, not sounds—

Bare as the conditions that required it

The unproven click of rudimentary tools—
Followed by arousal— commonly mistaken for confidence—

The only clarity no one is confused by—

"But proliferation replaces allure

That is how the dog and the scholar came to share the same sweater.

Or why I support the humans, if only out of expedience

It's a kind of naturalism.

Full of crude archaisms, neglected science.

Another caterwaul in the ungovernable tides.

Another swirl through the last resort.

"I myself have gone back to the ship unwilling to keep wandering the vertigo between corporation and contemplation—

But first we must address your misgivings.

That bones yodel and tide pools bark.

That I swoop from unmentioned trees and take a trout before retaking the limb

But my guess is that what really upsets you is the ancient context of vacancy

Where vacancy is rationality fatigued

But had you known that this was an amputation by transmutation—

I doubt you would have taken capsule full of fireflies.

Or heard the bird bones rattling in the clock.

Ranters, levelers, antinomians in the blood of the carp.

But for this you required cylinders, pulleys, and fulcrum

Until the circles conflate themselves with revelation, full of suddenly cold spots

The way a war resonates beside meat and shadow.

Because at this altitude, in this light

                  Hydrogen, oxygen no longer required—

"With my shelves full of finches and my drawers full of barnacles—

And though it is unfashionable, even offensive to invoke the instincts in an age of war—

I invoke them—neck high in the swollen tides—

I adjust the saw—

An act of scholarship so feral

Instinct is the origin.

Species is nothing.

Humbler arrangements farther on."

A note on the text:

In the years following the death of two of my dearest friends, I began this notebook with the idea that it would be the kind of correspondence or conversation that was no longer possible. I quickly discovered the theme of boredom and incompletion, which lies just behind loneliness. The notebook transformed into a journey, the traveler a kind of a contemporary Sisyphus, only I quickly discovered the limits of such a guide. At the point, the book began to collect the echoes of friends and poets, who have in some way served as guides, among them Dennis Phillips, Ray DiPalma, Robert Crosson, Laura Moriarty, and Paul Vangelisti, Amiri Baraka, Samuel Beckett.

Author Bio

Poet, essayist, and fiction writer, Standard Schafer's first book of poetry *Nova* was selected for the 1999 National Poetry Series and published by Sun & Moon Books. His second book, *Water & Power*, was published by Agincourt in 2005. *Desert Notebook* was published in Italy and the US in 2008 in limited editions. His poetry has been translated into Italian and anthologized internationally, most recently in *Nuova Poesia Americana* (Mondadori, 2005) as well as in Vol. 5 of *The PIP Anthology of World Poetry of the 20th Century* (Los Angeles: Green Integer, 2005). He has co-edited several literary and arts journals including *Ribot, New Review of Literature, Rhizome, The Feralist* and *Or*. His work has appeared in journals such as *Carolina Quarterly, New American Poetry, Aufgabe, Counter Punch* and *Slope*. He has taught writing and literature at Otis College of Art (Los Angeles)and California College of the Arts (San Francisco). He lives in Portland, Oregon, with his wife and daughter.

About Chax Press

Chax Press is a 501(c)(3) nonprofit organization, founded in 1984, and has published more than 140 books, including fine art and trade editions of literature and book arts works.

For more information, please see our web site at http://chax.org

Chax Press is supported by individual contributions, and by the Tucson Pima Art Council and the Arizona Commision on the Arts, with funds from the State of Arizona and the National Endowment for the Arts.

● ● ● ● TUCSON PIMA
● ● ◆ ● **A R T S**
● ● ● ● **C O U N C I L**

Arizona Commission on the Arts

N A T I O N A L
ENDOWMENT
FOR THE ARTS